AWESOME ACHIEVEMENT!

AWESOME ACHIEVEMENT!

Maximum Results in RSP

~

A Resource Specialist Guide

DR. SARAH SHABAZZ
Cover Art by Aminah ShaBazz
Edited by ShaVon Luckey

ShaBazz Enterprise Publishing

CONTENTS

I am dedicating this book to all the instructional aides and paraprofessionals who have worked with me over the last 24 years. Each of you have helped me become a better resource specialist and you have added to my effective teaching toolbox. Special thanks to Holly French, Tammie Forbes, Brenda Waddington, Jill Davey, Cheryl Marek, Anita Frias and Josephine Teece. You were the wind beneath my wings.

WHY I WROTE THIS BOOK

I wrote this book because I absolutely love what I do as a Resource Specialist. My favorite educational conference is the CARS+ (California Association of Resource Specialists and Special Educators) Conference. I have been presenting at the CARS+ Conference for the past three years and one day I decided that I should have a book to go along with my presentation. The book would be available to answer the questions I don't get to during the presentation. My conference titles have been, "Achieving Maximum Results in RSP", "Achieving Maximum Results in RSP with Distance Learning" and "Best Practices in RSP." These titles are skills that I developed over time, with trial, error, and discovering what works best. These best practices are based on my own personal teaching experiences that I have developed over the past 24 years. I would like to share this knowledge and my experiences with new and incoming Resource Specialists to give the opportunity to begin helping students right away, without having to take time to discover what works through trial and error. That has already been done.

"I appreciated the folder for each IEP goal with kid-friendly language to track progress."

"Dr. ShaBazz was a very inspirational speaker. The passion she has for teaching is easily conveyed through her session".

"I left feeling inspired and excited about the possibilities in RSP."

"I got some good ideas for my Learning Center. Thank you"

"I appreciated how honest, sincere, and organic the presentation was. You are genuine."

"Amazing information provided."

Introduction/Background Information

My first introduction to RSP was at the private Christian school that I attended in Los Angeles. At the time, I didn't know what it was. There was a teacher who came to the school twice a week. The teacher had a room where she would call children out of class and different students would go in and out all day. Many times, the students would come back to class with prizes, such as small toys or edible treats. Sometimes, they had parties and field trips that were exclusive to only to the students who went to the classroom. No one ever explained why these students went there. When I asked about going, I was told I could not. There were a few sets of siblings and they both went. Thinking back, this was definitely RSP.

For those of you who don't know or maybe have forgotten... RSP stands for Resource Specialist Program. The trained professional in the job position is skilled and equipped with strategies to support, empower, and enrich students with learning disabilities. Students with learning disabilities have processing deficits that makes it more difficult for them to learn. Sometimes concepts have to be presented several times and in different ways. These students experience difficulties with reading, writing, spelling, listening, speaking, mathematical computations or reasoning. Deficits vary and can be audio, visual or sensory, to name a few. A child with an auditory processing deficit has difficulty understanding what they hear. A child with a visual processing deficit has difficulty processing what they see. That can cause difficulty drawing or copying things down. They may also experience the inability to detect differences in letters or shapes and may often write some letters backwards (letter reversals). A child with a sensory processing disorder may experience discomfort from loud sounds, tags in their clothing, or feeling certain textures. All of these conditions can interfere with the learning process, making it more difficult to be successful with the core curriculum, without adult support and specialist academic instruction.

Examples of Learning Center Models

"Learning Center" is a word used to express the RSP model. I do not use "Learning Center"… I use **Achievement Center**. This name came about one year in 2004, when I wrote an email to inform the staff at the school where I'd work that the Learning Center would close forever on June 5th . I told them not to worry because we would be BAC (back) as the Brentwood Achievement Center in September. I felt like Achievement indicated success and to achieve is to succeed. Achievement is more powerful to me than just learning. Success center was another viable option.

Co-teaching is when there is a General Education teacher and a Special Education teacher teaching (both General Education and Special Education students) together in the same classroom. In some instances, instead of a Special Education teacher, an instructional assistant or para educator is the second adult in the classroom with the general education teacher.

I have personal experience teaching with this model. My first experience was me going into a general education high school biology class to support the students as an instructional assistant. I basically walked around and provided assistance as needed. I didn't really know if it was as effective as it could have been. Years later, I had the opportunity to team teach or co-teach as a teacher at an elementary school that "clustered" the students. Cluster means that all the RSP students were assigned to the same general education. There was a new 6th- grade teacher who had 14 RSP students on her roster. The majority of the RSP students had goals in reading, writing, and math, so it made sense and it was practical for her students to have in-class support all day. She was a great teacher with amazing classroom management, but math was not her strength. I taught the majority of the math lessons to all of the students. I showed each concept in two or three different ways to ensure that all students were able to understand what was being taught. That year the RSP students had a 15% increase in math on the state test. The model allowed the students to get exposure to the core math curriculum with support in the form of repetition, modeling, and immediate feedback.

The English Language Arts lessons were taught in the same manner. First, as a whole class lesson, then in small groups to provide extra support to the students who needed it. During that same time, I was also doing the same model in a fifth-grade classroom. I was working with a teacher who not only had a cluster of RSP students, he also had several Spanish Speaking Only students.

He literally repeated everything that he said in English in Spanish, for the Spanish-speaking students. School started in September back then. By January, the teacher didn't need to repeat everything in Spanish and rarely had to use Spanish at all. The next two years I looped with another teacher. Loop means to have the same class roster for two or more years. Research has shown that this is beneficial to the students and the students have more room and time for growth. One advantage is that the systems are already in place. The students know the expectations and the teacher knows the students' ability levels and needs. Because of this, time is not taken out to build those procedures that are already in place. This time can be used to work on learning new concepts and improving the academic skills needed for the students. This class was a fifth/sixth grade combo class the first year and the second year, it was a sixth grade class. A few new students were added, but it did not upset the system that was already in place. Two of the three teachers that I co-taught with went on to become principals and one of them was awarded "Teacher of the Year."

Centers is a model where students rotate every 15-20 minutes to work on various concepts usually with a teacher or paraprofessional. For example, centers can be set up where every center is a different subject or it can expand on the same concept with an extension to the same lesson. Centers can be set up with three, four, or five stations. Every station is a different lesson. Sometimes one center is for independent work where the student independently completes a writing assignment or a computer lesson.

Small Group is the most effective (according to research and experience) when there are less than five students. In the pull-out model, when students come into the resource room for instruction to work on their goals. There can be smaller groups or pairs within the small group. The students can be paired into two while the teacher works with one student.

Computer Based Learning is an option that entails having students use computer-based learning programs for a particular length of time on various concepts. There is a large range of programs available for students to use. Personally, I think that 20-minute sessions are sufficient for a (successful) computer program lesson. Thirty minutes can be a long time for some students and they can lose interest. A monitoring system should be in place for the student to track which programs they use for each setting. I also provide log-in and password information to the students so they can log in to each program, independently. Note: One of the downsides to using the computer is older students tend to find ways to access other programs such as YouTube, where they watch videos or play music in the background, instead of doing their assignments. Some schools have systems in place such as "GoGuardian," which allows the teacher to monitor what the student views on their computer and teachers can even log the student off inappropriate websites.

One-on-One instruction is when you, as the teacher (or your assistant), work(s) with one student on their own individual goals. Students usually make the most progress in this model. One-on-one instructions are not always available to all students due to the number of students needing help and the time allowed. Sometimes, it just so happens that the only time you can provide service is to a particular student. They may be the only student available at that time, due lunch scheduling and such.

Motivating Students to do Their Best

- Show students their goals. Students should know what their goals are. They need to know where they are functioning at this time, and where they should be. Write the goals down using kid-friendly language so that the child can understand them. For example: "I will count to 20 by myself and know the numbers when I see them."
- Have the students review their goals periodically, after working on them, to see if they are making progress and how much progress they have made and are making. Visual representation is a good way to show the child their progress. You do this by having a graph for them to color in, themselves or you can input the score into the computer to generate a graph.
- Self-Monitoring is done when the child monitors their own progress to see how they are doing and if they are making progress towards their goal(s).
- Decreased time in RSP. This is a good incentive for the student to spend more time with their grade-level peers. This is more important to the students when they get older. You will notice that 6th-grade girls prefer to spend as little time as possible in the Resource room. Achieving a goal is a great way for a student to gain the reward of decreased time in the Resource room. Sometimes students may have 60 or 90 minutes a day. You might be able to reduce their time to 30 minutes a day if they are making

adequate progress and noticeable improvement. Of course, they will have to reach all goals and be capable of being successful in the classroom without the support. Sometimes, putting students on the Watch and Consult model can be an incentive, as well. In this model, the student only consults with you at a given time once a week to let you know how they are doing in class and get any help they might need. You will also have to check in with the teacher weekly to ensure the student is staying on track. Sometimes if a student works hard enough, over time, they can be exited from RSP. When this happens, we have a big celebration and show all the other students that it is possible to graduate out of RSP. We go overboard by giving the students gift cards and treats from their Student Questionnaire form when they exit.

Keeping the Fun in Learning (Implementing Games)

- Scavenger Hunt – Create a fun worksheet to help the student identify the things in your classroom. Here are a few examples: A place where you go to sharpen your pencil. Where the books you use to look up the definitions of words are kept. Provide 15 to twenty different items and locations in the classroom that the students need to be aware of. It is a fun way to get accustomed to the layout and expectations of the room.
- Calming Environment – There should be a section, generally a corner where a student can go to calm down. This place can have alternative seating (yoga ball or bean bag chair) soft music or nature sounds, lavender or vanilla scents, stress balls, fidget toys, coloring sheets and cuddle toys. It should have partial privacy where the student is not out in the open and the teacher can keep an eye on them.
- Fidgets and Stress Relievers are good to have available for students. I have a large variety of them and the students can check them out for use. Some are more personalized and should only be used by one person. Others can be cleaned and sterilized between use and reused by other students. It is a quiet way to keep

students focused while fidgeting. Students need to be taught that once the item becomes a distractor it will be taken away.

- Some other useful items to have available for students are large rubber bands on the bottom of the chair legs to allow the student to fidget quietly with their feet. Bouncing their heels off the rubber bands can be soothing. Velcro strips on the underside of the desk are also a quiet fidget device. The student can feel the roughness with their fingers out of sight. Cell phone pop grips, which are usually placed on the back of a cell phone to hold it easier, are also a good fidget device. They are usually collapsible and can go up and down. They can be positioned on the desktop where the students will have access to use it quietly without distracting other students.

- You might have students who love to tap, knock, bump and bam. You know the ones who are always drumming on something? Well, I give them a mouse pad to use for drumming purposes and they are only allowed to drum on it with the eraser side of two unsharpened pencils. This way they can get their drumming out, it doesn't distract anyone, and I don't have to hear it.

Overlays and Specialty Paper

- Overlays are a paper-sized transparent sheet used to lay on top of whatever text the student is reading. The colors are usually soft pastels. There is a wide range of hues from ivory to gray. I have been using overlays for students ever since I started teaching elementary-age students. Many times, students either had it on their IEPs or transferred into our school with the accommodation already on their IEPs. Whenever this happened, I was sure to provide the teacher with an overlay in the color indicated by the IEP so that the student would have access to it while they are in their general education class since they spend the majority of the day there doing class work. Just to let you know, it is a good idea to have several of the same colors because student and teacher both seem to never return them. Once, when I was at a conference, I met a nice woman representing a company. She was at a booth and provided me with a full set of all the colors, for no cost! I was grateful because over the years I had lost several colors due to them not being returned to me. I do not know a particular company in the U.S. that specializes in color overlays (I know that there are a few in the U.K). You can easily find a variety of cover overlay choices by searching for "color overlay for reading" or "color overlays for dyslexia" on Amazon.com.

- Specialty Paper is paper that is made to assist students with difficulty writing on regular lined paper. Some specialized paper is made with boxes for the student to write a letter in each box or help with proper spacing. Some papers have raised lines to help the student (good for visually impaired students as well) to stay on the line. There is also paper that is highlighted. Specialty Paper can be purchased from the "Mead Paper Company." There is a company online, "nationalautismresources.com," that sells raised-lined paper. Another company, "teacherspapteachers.com," sells a few different options for highlighted paper. They call this adapted paper. There is also "especialneeds.com," which has an adaptive paper that is a little more costly. A company named "Pacon" sells a multi-sensory raised lined paper that can be purchased on Amazon. I am sure there are other companies out there as well. These are the ones that I am familiar with.

- Game-related learning is a way to have fun while learning. There are games on the market for every concept imaginable; place value, fractions, multiplication, affixes, parts of speech, and sentences, just to give you an idea. You can purchase such games online or from a teacher supply store, such as Lakeshore. Games can also be made. I remember when I was in my teaching program, we had to make board games out of manila folders envelopes which we called folder games. The game pieces like the tokens and cards are kept in a small envelope that is glued to the outside of the folder and the name of the game is on the tab. When the folder is open there is a game board covering both sides of the opened folder. These games can be made specifically for whatever concept you want the students to practice. Games are a fun way to engage the students while reviewing and reinforcing a learned concept.

- BAM is a great game that can be made for any concept. The object of the game is to pull a card and read it. It can either be a concept card (one might ask what is 3x5 or "make a sentence out of the word forever") or an action card, which might say "give your opponent 5 pts, compliment your neighbor, get out of BAM or even BAM. When a student gets a BAM card, they lose all their cards. The game is very engaging and the students learn while they play. The most fun is the action cards because you never know what you are going to have to do. We found the game online and adapted it to meet the needs of our students.

- Moving and Motion is a great way to make learning fun. Some of the kinesthetic movements that are paired with learning certain concepts make it fun to learn and easy to remember. There are a lot of things out there that you can use. Ortin Gillingham uses tapping and pounding to assist with decoding and encoding. You can always make things up as you go to add to your toolbox of movements and motions, in learning.

- Technology is one of the best ways to keep students engaged. In the time we are living in, technology has taken over the baby rattle and other such toys. Babies are engaged at a young age and can maneuver the screen to keep themselves entertained. The colors, sounds, and immediate feedback make it harder for students to be interested in plain white pages with black text. Technology can be used in many ways, even for games. Kahoot! is a highly engaging game that allows the students to answer questions using their computer, tablet, Chromebook, or phone. Jeopardy can also be played this way. Students can participate in polls, do interactive worksheets, and a wide variety of educational computer programs.

Managing Behavior

- Building Relationships is the first step to managing behavior. Your students need to know that you care. Nel Nodding is an expert on care in education and she insists that students thrive when they know the educator cares. I know from experience that students will learn and will give their all when they feel that their teacher cares about them. On the other hand, students will resist, refuse to do their work, and not follow directions when they feel that the teacher does not care for them. Building a relationship can happen quickly with just a few minutes every day. Whenever I get a new student, I call the student for a "get-acquainted" meeting. I ask them about their previous school, explain how the program works, and welcome them. I always start with the Student Questionnaire. I have one on file for each student.
- The Student Questionnaire is a form I created to ask the students about their favorite things. I ask about their favorite color, movie, music, chips, candy, ice cream, and restaurant. I ask them what they want to do when they grow up, if they have any pets, and what sports and activities they enjoy most. Sometimes it is best if the adult writes the answers for the student. Many of them struggle with spelling or with writing itself. I use the Student Questionnaire to build a rapport. Students get excited if you remember that they like the color blue or that they play on a

14

baseball team. It also works well for raffle prizes, or when a student has an exit party for testing out of RSP.

- Teaching procedures ensure that the students know what your expectations are. Be sure to explain your expectations on the first day. If you don't want students to wear caps or chew gum in your room, make sure you let them know the first time they come in. If you let them do it the first time, they will assume it is acceptable and it will be harder to get them to understand that it is not.

- Review the behavior expectations with the students. Make sure they know and understand what you expect and why.

- Have each student explain the expectations to you in their own words. This is to ensure that they know what the expectations are, so later you won't have to guess if they understood the expectations, in the event they break a rule. I have the students rewrite a paragraph entitled "Why I am here" in their own handwriting, then we read it together. The paper explains that the student is there to work on and improve their goals.

- Talk it out when students are frustrated. Have them express their feelings (when they are ready). Sometimes you must allow them time to cool down, calm down, and feel like talking. When the student talks to you, listen. Let them know that you are paying attention. Respond with reassuring head nodding and verbal affirmation, "I see" and "I understand." Paraphrase what the student says to show understanding.

- There are several behavior theme book sets available, Quill.com has "MySELF." This is a set of 12 books with titles such as: "I can be kind," "I can stay calm," and "I can follow the rules." My favorite is the "Let's Talk About" series by Joy Berry. I used these for my own kids many years ago. Then there are also some individual books like *My Mouth is a Volcano* and *What if Everybody Did That?*

- "What Bugs Me" – is a writing assignment that supports a child in writing down their feelings to express the things that upset or frustrates them. It is best if it is done with the support of an adult. This has proven to be a very effective activity.

- When a student has ADD or ADHD (even when it is un-diagnosed) sometimes they just have extra energy to burn. My assistant came up with an obstacle course in our classroom. I had brought my agility ladder from my home gym for the students to use in the classroom, but then I took it back home. To impro-vise, she made a zig-zag obstacle course on the floor using blue tape. I left my peddler in the classroom for the students to use. She also made sensory binds where she hid small toys in beans. She then laminated a checklist for the students to check off the items as they are found. She also made a dew carnival-style game where the student had to throw a large dice or a soft ball into a bucket or bin. One of the fun things she did was make targets on the whiteboard. Each target had a sight word written inside. The student had to throw a soft dart to hit the word. If they hit the word, they had to spell the word and then write the word on a list on the side of the board. These types of activities keep the student busy, moving, and learning at the same time.

Rewarding Students' Success

- Incentives (Raffle Tickets/Treasure box)- Give out raffle tickets to students following rules and completing their assignments. Have a weekly drawing and have the student choose a prize from the prize or treasure box. "Wheel of Names" and "Picker Wheel" are electronic methods of randomly choosing a name.
- Verbal praise and recognition are always good ways to acknowledge students making progress and/or good choices. Call out their name so that everyone can hear, and say for example, "I want to let you all know that Veronica increased her words per minute by 10 words this week," "Jeffery has learned his 4 times table with 100% accuracy," "Coleen is my only student who has had perfect attendance since the beginning of the year," "David has had perfect attendance this whole week" (for a student who struggles with attendance). Give them their accolades and watch them beam with pride.

Measuring Student Progress

Frequent Progress Monitoring is important to track student success (or lack thereof). It is a great way to measure progress and to let the students see what progress they are making. It also alerts you to make changes to the study plan if adequate progress is not being made. I like to monitor progress every two weeks for the first six months of school and then monthly, after that. I reward progress by providing an extra raffle ticket for the week. It increases the student's chances of winning.

Showing progress on a chart or graph gives the student a visual to see the progress that is being made. It is easier to see the line climbing upwards on a chart than it is to only hear about it. Seeing it makes it real for the student. It helps them to better understand the growth that they are making.

Have students review their own work and discuss their progress. Ask them questions such as:

- What is your goal?
- Have you met your goal?
- What do you need to do to meet your goal?
- How can I help you?

Strategies for Learning

In the first book I wrote, *A Parent's Guide to Making Every Child a Reader*, I provided a list of strategies to use to improve reading for students experiencing reading difficulty. I am going to refer you to that book rather than restate the same information again, here. I will say, be sure to review vocabulary before reading a story and make sure the students understand what the words mean. I tell stories and give examples to make sure the student can relate to what I am explaining to them.

Parents often ask if I can help their students with dyslexia. Dyslexia is a reading disorder.

People with Dyslexia have difficulty reading. They usually read slower and take more time to read something. Because of this, they often avoid reading. If something is read to them, they usually understand it and have no problem with comprehension. Dyslexia doesn't go away, but you can use strategies to make reading easier. That is why I use audiobooks for my students. I like the student to either have a PDF copy or a book to follow along with the audio. I also have my students read stories or books that are fun or interesting to them. This year my fourth-grade students read *Tales of a Fourth Grade Nothing* and *Fourth Grade Rats*. When we learned about multiple-meaning words we read *Amelia Bedelia* books and reviewed the words in the book that had multiple meanings.

Teaching Reading

Reading is my passion. I tried to get as much training in reading as possible because I wanted to know everything about teaching reading. I usually began by assessing the students to see where they are in reading. My assessment lets me know if the student has phonemic awareness, knows phonics, can decode, has fluency, and comprehends what they read. When it comes to teaching reading, I do not use a one-size fits all method. I give the students what they are lacking to make them proficient readers. Phonemic awareness is hearing the syllables in a word, rhyming words, and segmenting words. Some people say it is the part of reading that you can do in the dark. You don't have to see phonemic awareness to show you have it. Some students do not have phonemic awareness, not because they never learned it, but because they never will. It is missing. It may be missing due to a learning deficit. Even without phonemic awareness, a student can still learn to read. For these students, I teach them with repetition and memorization. "Edmark" is a program that supports students needing to learn to read this way.

For students needing to learn to read and spell multisyllabic words, I use "R.E.W.A.R.D.S", a multisyllabic word reading strategy system. It is scripted and comes with a teacher and a student book. "LiPS" is a system used to teach reading and spelling beginning with phonics. It teaches the vowel circle which includes the 23 vowel sounds (long and short) and the vowel combinations. Ortin Guillingham is a multi-sensory method of learning reading with includes using sand, textures, tapping, and pounding to teach reading and spelling. The student needs to be able to read at a mid-second grade level before using this program. For students needing fluency, I use "Read Naturally." It uses repeated practice readings after listening to the passage being read. It goes from kindergarten level to eight-grade. All the passages are non-fiction, so the student learns about many things as they improve their reading fluency. The "Language! Live" program can be used for students in middle school and above. I am of the firm belief that struggling readers need 90 minutes of reading each day. At least half of it should be structured reading, by getting explicit reading instructions and by having guided reading from an adult. The remaining reading can be listening to and following along with an audiobook or using a computer program. I don't recommend silent sustained reading for students who struggle with reading. They need guidance. Without guidance, they will miscall words, skip words, or not read at all.

Teaching Math

Of course, math begins with learning numbers, counting, identifying, one-to-one correspondence, and writing. Once that is mastered you move along to place values, addition, subtraction, and so on. I always teach all my students, regardless of their grade, money, measurement, time, and roman numerals. Why? Because it is everyday life and they need to know the value of a dime, how many days there are in a month, what time it is on an analog clock, and other things that they will come in contact with commonly. I used to spend a lot of time trying to get students to learn multiplication facts. Now we go over them, but I don't expect them to learn them before we move on in math. I provide them with a multiplication chart. I specifically use the one provided in WebIEP, which is approved for the state test. Up until the 2021/2022 school year, it only went up to 9 x 9. It now goes up to 12 x 12. I usually copy it on colored paper and laminate it. I put the student's IEP so they can use the multiplication chart for homework, classwork, test, and quizzes. I teach them to use multiplication charts. This way, the student can compute grade-level math beginning in fourth grade. They can do long division, multi-digit multiplication, and other math. Eventually, by looking up the same thing over and over, they will learn them. Meanwhile, they are not stifled doing only addition and subtraction while learning the multiplication facts (which they may never learn). Using the multiplication chart leveled the playing field in math for many of the RSP students. I consider it a real breakthrough. We have a print-rich environment in the classroom. Here are several colorful wall charts with various math concepts that the student can see and review. We also have manipulatives of various kinds and many math games. We use cards, dominoes, and dice to help build and support the student's math skills. Dominoes and dice can be used for subertizing (knowing the number of dots instantly by seeing them). Cards and dice can be used for less than or greater than and the addition, subtraction, multiplication, and division math facts.

Teaching Writing (Written Language)

I like to teach that writing is talking written down. I have the student tell me their thoughts and then have them write what they said. I usually write it for them in the beginning. We also do a lot of guided writing. We use "Thinking Maps" (a type of graphic organizer) and sentence frames. That is when you provide the structure of the sentences and students only have to provide some of the information to complete the assignment. The more practice that the students get with sentence frames, the less information the teacher provides. I always use a word bank for each writing assignment to encourage students to use correct spelling. Spelling is part of writing. I like the Rebecca Sitton method of ensuring that the student can write frequently used words and sight words in their writing. Orton Gillingham encourages that also. They call them "Red words" and the students keep a "Red word" journal of the words they have learned to spell to use for their writing. Personal dictionaries are also a favorite writing support that I use. This is a blank alphabetized booklet where the student can write down words that they use in their writing. I usually write a few words in the booklet before giving the booklet to the students. I write "animal" on page A, "because" on the B page, "cousin" and "children" on the C page, and so on. Daily writing is a great way to encourage writing. I like to have the students come in while the music is playing, get their journals, sit down, and begin writing from the writing prompt on the board. Most students do not want to share, but some want to share every day. I allow those who want to share and don't force the ones who do not want to share. We (my assistant or I) read the writings and make corrections for the students to review to help them prevent the same errors in the future. After writing about five assignments, we have the student choose one of their writings to rewrite and make error-free. These writings go into a different journal. The first journal is a folder with notebook paper held by brads and the second journal is a real writing journal. I like to do fun writing assignments. Here a few examples: Where did you get your name? What is the most fun you ever had? Describe your favorite movie. So, at the end, they have a book of well-written assignments that they can show and be proud of. The students always ask to take them home at the end of the year, which I allow.

Virtual Learning with RSP

Engagement! Engagement! Engagement is the key to having a successful virtual class! Basically, you begin the same way that you would with an in-person class. Before the first day of class, I send an introductory text to all parents. I let them know that this is my cell phone (you can use Google Voice or Class Dojo if you prefer). My cell phone works best for me. It is the same number that I provide to my tutoring clients, so parents are calling me on that number all the time. I let the parents know that I sent a zoom link invite to their child via Google Classroom and the days and times that I will be working with their child. On the first day of virtual class after I introduce myself, I begin by explaining my expectations: I show them to the students so that they can read along as I discuss them. There is a lot of screen-sharing when teaching online. All Cameras On. No exceptions. "I cannot teach you if I can't see you. If your camera is off, you will be placed in the waiting room while I notify your parent that you are not following the rules. I don't know what your other teachers' rules are, but these are my rules. I need you to follow them so you can learn the best you can."

Mics must be muted unless you are speaking or told to unmute. Raise your hand to speak. Sit upright in a chair. No laying down in bed. Be in a quiet location without distractions. No little kids or pets unless we are doing a show and share. No eating. If you must go to the restroom let me know in the chat. No side conversations in the chat. Speak kind words and be respectful of everyone. Come prepared with a pencil and paper or a whiteboard and marker. Pay attention and participate.

I review the students' goals with them in a one-on-one setting and send a folder (with their kid-friendly goals written on the inside flap of the folder) home for them. The work provided is related to the student's goals. Some parents take pictures and send me the work that way, others exchange folders with me when I provide new work. If I have three students and they all have the same goals I might say, "All of you have goals to learn how to compute two-step word problems, so we are going to work on that today." I will then show a YouTube video, first. I like short videos that are only two or three minutes. Then, I show them how to do some problems on the whiteboard while sharing my screen. After that, I display problems for them to do themselves. They either put the answer in the chat or hold up their whiteboard for me to see. I can't usually see what they write on paper with a pencil. Sometimes we read class chapter books by having the pdf on the screen while listening to the audiobook. We review the list of vocabulary words on the screen and discuss the definitions before reading the chapter. After reading the chapter we discuss it and write a few sentences. For writing, we use "Thinking Maps" (Graphic Organizers) and a lot of sentence frames in the beginning until they can write independently. We show a lot of concepts by using Youtube videos, first, before working on the concept as a class.

I call on students randomly to participate, making sure that all students are called upon. So far, my largest class has consisted of eight students. Some classes have five, three, or only one student. Sometimes we split the class and my assistant has some of the students in the breakout room. Other times, she may only work with one student who needs a reading assessment or needs more help on a concept. When we were doing Distance Learning during the Pandemic, I would go into the General Education Teacher's Zoom meeting and have the teacher put me and the RSP student(s) in a Breakout room. I called that the "Virtual Push-in Model."

We have fun things woven into our instructional time. On Mondays, we talk about our weekend. On Tuesday, we have a Kahoot! Game, to review the previous week's lessons. On Wednesday, we do a scavenger hunt. On Thursday, we have our raffle. We use the wheel of names. We choose two students from each class; three students are chosen if either me or my assistant are out that day.   I show a few choices of prizes for them to choose from if they win the raffle.

I know some teachers didn't care for virtual learning but, let it be known that I LOVE teaching online. My PhD was done completely on-line except for the four-day residencies that I had in person. I had also been teaching online college classes since 2017 at a teacher prep college. I volunteered to continue teaching the elementary school students on IEPs who didn't come back to school in the district where I work. I made it fun and engaging and the students look forward to our sessions.

Teaching High School RSP

Most of the activities and strategies in this book can also be used for older students. My very first teaching assignment was teaching high school. The school was departmentalized for special ed meaning, there was a special ed teacher that taught each of the core subjects. I taught 9th grade English my first year. We had special education teachers for science, social studies, and math. The students on P.E. (Physical Education), lunch time and electives along with the other students.

This is how I taught my English class. First I found out what the other English teachers were teaching and I taught the same thing at a lever that my student could comprehend. For instance, when the other students read Romeo and Juliet: we read Romeo and Juliet also. It did my heart good when I overheard students talking about how they had discussed the plot with one of their (non-special ed) peers. I did not use the grade level text. I used the same story, but I presented it on a lower reading level so that the students were able to read and be successful in understanding the content. We discussed the meanings of different words and phrases because Shakespearean language can be difficult to understand. It is not the same as standard American English. As the general ed students read various novels, I would find something similar and have my students read it. I had subscribed to a magazine called Storyworks. Sometimes it had plays for the students to read (an act out) from recent movies. There have been times where I rewrote the text myself to make it easier for my students to comprehend. Rewriting Shakespeare's plays in standard English is no easy task, but it was important to me that my students understood the literature.

There were some tasks considered life skills that I thought all student should be able to perform. I made sure to teach these concepts to my English students. One such task was learning to write their first and last names in cursive. This armed them with a signature and they were able to sign their name if needed. I also had an activity sheet where they would identify different parts of a newspaper and understand vocabulary such as byline and headline. We also had a day without electronics worksheets where the students would have to start in the morning and go the whole entire day without using any electronic device. Basically they were not able to use a Computer, tablet or smartphone to help them to get their answers. So they would start off in the morning and they would have a list of things to do. The task included finding a dog doctor, they would have to use the Yellow Pages for that. They would also need to know to look for it under, veterinarian. They had to find a television show at 3 o'clock for a three year old to watch, and it cannot be a talk show or soap opera. They had to locate a particular country on a map, find out the best time to plant carrots, look up a word in the dictionary, look up the event in an encyclopedia and find a recipe for chocolate chip cookies. In the process of doing this activity worksheet they had to use a yellow page, white pages, TV guide, a thesaurus, dictionary, encyclopedia, atlas, and an almanac.

I had my seniors complete a voter registration form application. I also had my male students learn about and understand the selective service process. I explained to them how it was something that they had to do at the age of 18 and that they would be penalized if they did not get it done. They would not be able to go to college and get financial aid if the form is not completed. I feel like life skills are a very big part of education. Sometimes I would have students ask me why are we doing these types of assignments in English class. I said you're doing it because it's something that you need to know and I want to make sure that you know it, so I'm teaching you myself. I taught my high school students to tell time, count money, identify and count with the Roman numerals and I also taught the measurements. To teach the measurements, I actually have empty containers from half a pint size up to a gallon so that they can actually see the physical dimensions of the measurement units we were speaking of.

Most of the things that I did for my elementary school students, were also affected for the high school students. The older students need to know some additional concepts, such as completing a job application, which is something we also did. We did mock interviews and sometimes we sat around and had discussions. We would turn our desk around in a circle and have a roundtable discussion on various subjects. We did not do this often, but it did occur from time to time. One topic I remember discussing was if there should be Black History Month and why. Some of the students were very passionate about their perspectives. At the end when it was all over everyone accepted the opinion of the other person even if they did not agree.

One of the first assignments I had my English students do was write a letter to someone that they had not seen since school ended in June. In the letter, they had to explain what they did during the summer and what they expected from high school. I also had them address an envelope. They were not given any directions. This assignment result was quite comical. Some of the students had telephone numbers on the envelopes. Some of them did not understand how or where to write their name and address. Others did not know their own addresses and did not know they needed to use a ZIP Code. They did not know how to write city, comma, state. This assignment taught me a lot about where they were and how much support they needed.

Since we were not departmentalized, I only taught English my first year, and did not have the opportunity to teach math. However, in my third year I did teach science to students in SDC. Had I taught math, I would've allowed the students to use the state approved multiplication table that is in the CAASPP test. I also would have taught them to use a calculator by providing calculator assignments that required them to compute various math problems. We would've thoroughly reviewed how to break down a word problem knowing when to add, subtract, multiply or divide. I would've started at the basics and worked towards mastery. When I teach math I teach concepts by modeling and practicing then providing independent practice. The next day after that concept has been learned I give the student two problems of the same concept. If they get both problems right, we can move on to the next concept. If they miss a problem they get two more problems. So every problem they miss they get two more problems. This helps the students to apply themselves, try their best to pay attention and understand the concept being taught.

Just keep in mind that high school students are just big little kids. They want acknowledgement and acceptance. Build a rapport with them. Some of the concepts used for younger students can also be used for the bigger kids. They love Kahoot, and Jeopardy. They usually like bingo and Bam. Some of them get excited about stickers or happy faces on their work. Believe it or not, quite a few of them also enjoy coloring. It seems to be relaxing for them. Journal writing is good for high school students. I always gave them a writing prompt every day. I tried to make them interesting. One time the topic was what would you do if you found a wallet with $500 in it ? What would you do if you found a baby on your doorstep? What would you do if your best friend told you she was pregnant? I tried to make the topics fun and relatable. I remember, one of the students said that they would look at the baby and if it was cute they would keep it, but if it wasn't cute they would put it on the neighbors doorstep. Most of the students said they would take the baby to the mom and call the authorities to see what they need to do with the baby. Some of them said they would keep the baby. I really enjoyed teaching high school RSP. I came very close to getting that opportunity again. That option presented itself at the same exact time my opportunity for becoming a full-time college professor came about and I chose to go with the college level students. I happen to have several currently enrolled high school students in my classes.

I think departmentalizing Special Education was a great idea. The Special Education students' schedules look just like the General Education students' schedules. They were not in the same classroom all day. Even on the SDC level, the students have different teachers. Once when we had a fire drill one my students refused to come and stand with me and my class. Later she told me, " Everyone knows you teach Special Ed and I didn't want to be associated with you". So, she went and stood with another class. That same student put her notebook up one day when someone entered the room. She held her notebook up in front of her face, so that the person would not be able to see her. After the person left the room, I reminded her that she had an 8 x 10 glossy of herself in the front of her notebook.

I really enjoyed teaching high school RSP. Just like the younger students, it is important for students to know why they are there. They need to know what their goals are and work towards them.

Organization is key. With five different periods of students it was very important to have a system in place. What I did was use a different color folder for each period. So, if a student had a green folder that meant they were in my third period class. If a student had a red folder they would be in my sixth period class. I had a different color for each. This was very effective.

Message to a New First Time RSP Teacher

For the first time in over 24 years, I am returning to work after summer break in a different position. I will no longer be working as a Resource Specialist. This is what I would tell the teacher who takes on my previous position (I didn't use the word replace or replacement, because I consider myself irreplaceable. LOL). First, I want to say congratulations and good luck! You are embarking on an incredible journey. Your job is to provide the needed resources to students as well as provide suggestions to teachers to assist students who may not be on your caseload. That was something no one told me and I did not know when I started out in this position. Staff will look to you for answers and you need to have them. Learn everything you can about strategies to help students be successful.

I never start services until the first day of the third week of school. The first two weeks of school are spent meeting with students individually, doing assessments, preparing IEP at a Glance forms for the general education teachers, collaborating and planning with the "Para", contacting parents, updating the master IEP/Tri schedule, meeting with the school psychologist and IEP team members, and scheduling.

When scheduling, keep in mind you should not schedule students doing lunch, recess, P.E. or designated fun time like Fun Friday. You want the students to apply themselves and do their best work. They will not perform well if they are crying or upset because they are missing a fun activity. If the general education teacher is showing a movie, allow the students to see the movie and have them make up the session with you at a different time.

When you prepare your IEP at a Glance decide which form you prefer to use, I like the one-page model. Sometimes, the computer generates a four-page document called IEP at a Glance. In my opinion, that is not a glance. I prefer to make my own rather than use the computer generated one. Please be sure to prepare a log to have the General Education Teacher sign and date when they receive their copy of the IEP at a Glance. I had to start doing this because I have always provided this information to the teachers at the beginning of the year and any time a new student transferred in or had an initial IEP meeting. After the second occurrence, when I had a teacher say I never gave them the IEP at a Glance (which I had), I began having them sign for it and I never had anyone say they never got it or didn't know anything about it. I attended a training once which was called, "If it was not written down, it didn't happen". Be sure to document everything!

One thing I would encourage you to do is make a spreadsheet. When I started out I used to draw it out by hand using a ruler to make the grid and then writing in the information. As the years passed, I began using an electronic spreadsheet, which is more efficient. The spreadsheet should include all of the following: student name, birthday, age, grade, parent/guardian name, address, telephone number, disability code, other services and goals. You could also have a place for notes such as special accommodations. This document may take a while to compile, but the results will be well worth the time spent compiling. Any time any situation arises you will have the information at your fingertips, or at least in arms reach. I usually print off the most up-to-date copy and keep it in a folder in my top desk drawer. I remember once about 22 years ago; I was the summer school teacher for Extended School Year (ESY) also called "Special Education Summer School." The director of pupil services was my supervisor for the summer session. She came to visit one day during the summer session and while I was busy at the front of the room with the students, she went over to my desk, lifted, and viewed my handmade spreadsheet. I witnessed her broad smile that I knew was a seal of approval. This was my first time using a spreadsheet for RSP. I had decided to use one because I had students from throughout the school district and I was not readily aware of their information or needs. I have been using a spreadsheet ever since and it has been very beneficial. This past school year, when I was the Independent Study RSP teacher for 13 schools in the district, having a spreadsheet was a lifesaver. I don't think I could have survived the school year without it.

Lean on your Para for support. Many of them have built a wealth of knowledge over the years by watching and learning from experienced Special Education teachers and have dealt with a variety of academic needs and discipline situations. Value your Para! They are your greatest support system. They are your personal cheerleader, your partner in crime, and they can be your friend. You will become in tunes with each other and have the same relationship as red beans and rice, peanut butter and jelly or fish and chips. If someone sees one of you, they will ask about the other one. Please build a rapport with your Para. Find out what they like and give them small gifts and tokens of appreciation, just because.

On a closing note, you have what you need. Go out there and be great!

CONTACT INFORMATION

- Email: sshabazzphd@gmail.com
- Phone: (760) 900-5850
- Name: Dr. Sarah ShaBazz
- Address: P.O. Box 1753 Victorville, CA 92393
- Website: www.drsarahshabazz.com
- @SarahUgwumba on Twitter
- @Drsarahshabazz on Instagram

OTHER BOOKS BY THE AUTHOR

A Parents Guide to Making Every Child A Reader
Awesome Achievement! The Companion Packet
So Many Books
So Many More Books
Two Grand
Arielle's Two Grand
Modern Medicine
The Kwanzaa Family
The Name Game

www.ingramcontent.com/pod-product-compliance
Lightning Source LLC
Chambersburg PA
CBHW060356130626
46553CB00003B/1261

* 9 7 9 8 9 8 6 8 2 6 3 0 1 *